HILLARY
CLINTON

Groundbreaking Politician

BY JUDY DODGE CUMMINGS

CONTENT CONSULTANT
DR. ANDRA GILLESPIE
ASSOCIATE PROFESSOR OF POLITICAL SCIENCE
EMORY UNIVERSITY

Essential Library
An Imprint of Abdo Publishing | abdopublishing.com

abdopublishing.com

Published by Abdo Publishing, a division of ABDO, PO Box 398166, Minneapolis, Minnesota 55439. Copyright © 2017 by Abdo Consulting Group, Inc. International copyrights reserved in all countries. No part of this book may be reproduced in any form without written permission from the publisher. Essential Library™ is a trademark and logo of Abdo Publishing.

Printed in the United States of America, North Mankato, Minnesota
112016
092016

THIS BOOK CONTAINS
RECYCLED MATERIALS

Cover Photo: Gage Skidmore/Alamy
Interior Photos: Bill Clark/CQ Roll Call/AP Images, 4; Seth Wenig/AP Images, 7; Reiri Kurihara/Yomiuri Shimbun/AP Images, 9; Clinton Presidential Library, 12, 17, 18, 26, 32, 42; Lee Balterman/The LIFE Picture Collection/Getty Images, 22; John M. Hurley/Boston Globe/Getty Images, 28; Wally McNamee/Corbis Historical/Getty Images, 37; Donald R. Broyles/AP Images, 46; Stephan Savoia/AP Images, 51; Doug Mills/AP Images, 52, 63; Ken Goldman/AP Images, 56; Ajit Kumar/AP Images, 61; Bebeto Matthews/AP Images, 66; Dusan Vranic/AP Images, 73; Charlie Neibergall/AP Images, 74; Amel Emric/AP Images, 78; Barbara Kinney/WireImage/Getty Images, 81; Pete Souza/The White House/AP Images, 83; Patrick Semansky/AP Images, 90; Andrew Harnik/AP Images, 95

Editor: Amanda Lanser
Series Designer: Becky Daum

Publisher's Cataloging-in-Publication Data

Names: Cummings, Judy Dodge, author.
Title: Hillary Clinton: groundbreaking politician / by Judy Dodge Cummings.
Description: Minneapolis, MN : Abdo Publishing, [2017] | Series: Essential lives | Includes bibliographical references and index.
Identifiers: LCCN 2016942706 | ISBN 9781680783018 (lib. bdg.) | ISBN 9781680774818 (ebook)
Subjects: LCSH: Clinton, Hillary Rodham, 1947- --Juvenile literature. | Presidents' spouses--United States--Biography--Juvenile literature. | Women cabinet officers--United States-- Biography--Juvenile literature. | Cabinet officers--United States--Biography--Juvenile literature. | United States. Department of State--Biography--Juvenile literature. | Women legislators--United States--Biography--Juvenile literature. | Legislators--United States--Biography--Juvenile literature. | United States. Congress. Senate--Biography --Juvenile literature. | Women presidential candidates--United States--Biography--Juvenile literature. | Presidential candidates--United States--Biography--Juvenile literature.
Classification: DDC 973.929/092 [B]--dc23
LC record available at http://lccn.loc.gov/2016942706

CONTENTS

CHAPTER
ONE

SHATTERING
THE GLASS CEILING

I t was standing-room only in the Wells Fargo Center in Philadelphia, Pennsylvania, on July 28, 2016. A huge screen hung behind a stage bedecked with digital American flags. Professional politicians in suits mingled with Americans of different ages, races, and ethnicities, some in jeans and T-shirts, others sporting patriotic bling. These delegates had gathered at the Democratic National Convention to watch history being made.

Since 1832, members of the Democratic Party have met every four years to choose a presidential candidate. The difference in 2016 was the gender of the person being selected. For the first time in US history, a major political party nominated a woman—Hillary Rodham Clinton.

Hillary Clinton accepted her nomination at the Democratic National Convention on July 28, 2016.

In It to Win It

Clinton's nomination was a moment that had begun more than a year earlier. On April 12, 2015, people from all walks of life appeared on a video on Clinton's website. They discussed their future plans—have a baby, start a business, go to college. At the end of the video, Clinton announced: "I'm getting ready to do something, too. I'm running for president."[1] So began her 2016 campaign.

Clinton's first challenge was to win her party's nomination. At first, she had five competitors, all men. But within eight months, only Clinton and Vermont Senator Bernie Sanders remained standing.

Sanders gave Clinton a fight she had not expected. His call for a political revolution

FEEL THE BERN

Bernie Sanders, an independent senator from Vermont, gained a large following among progressive voters. He built his campaign around economic and political reforms, including a higher minimum wage, free college tuition, and an end to the close relationship between politicians and Wall Street lobbyists. When Clinton secured the Democratic nomination for the presidency, Sanders used the momentum of his campaign to influence the Democratic Party's platform at the national convention. The platform included many of the reforms Sanders had promised during his campaign, such as a higher minimum wage and free college tuition for some students.

Over the course of the primary season, Clinton and Sanders debated nine times.

appealed to many young adults and progressives in the Democratic Party. Despite Sanders's popularity with these groups of voters, Clinton's early lead in the popular vote was too large for him to overcome. Even before the primary season ended, Clinton had clinched the Democratic nomination. Sanders endorsed her on July 12, 2016.

Running Mate

The choice of a running mate is one of the first presidential decisions a candidate makes. On July 22, 2016, Clinton selected Virginia governor Tim Kaine as her vice-presidential pick.

Kaine is a longtime politician. A former civil rights lawyer, he served as the mayor of Richmond, Virginia, and as both lieutenant governor and governor of that state before being elected to the US Senate in 2012. During an interview on the television program *60 Minutes*, Clinton explained why she chose Kaine as her running mate. She said, "the most important qualification is that the person . . . be ready to become president."[2] She wanted someone who could step into her shoes at a moment's notice. She believed Kaine was that man.

Political analysts believed there was another reason why Clinton picked Kaine as her vice president. They suggested Clinton chose Kaine because he is a middle-aged white man who has moderate political positions. He could help Clinton attract independent and Republican voters who were uncomfortable voting for the Republican nominee, businessman and former reality television star Donald Trump.

Stronger Together

On July 28, the last night of the Democratic convention, speaker after speaker proclaimed Clinton's virtues and

Clinton announced Tim Kaine as her running mate on July 23, 2016.

decried Trump's flaws. Finally, the time arrived for the nominee to address the crowd.

Rachel Platten's "Fight Song" played in the background as Clinton walked onto the stage to accept the nomination. The pop song had become Clinton's anthem on the campaign trail. Clinton waved to a crowd that roared its approval back.

In her nomination speech, Clinton both acknowledged people's concerns and extolled America's virtues. It was true, she admitted, that economic and social inequality and threats at home and abroad still existed. But, she insisted, "Don't let anyone tell you that our country is weak; we're not. Don't let anyone tell you that we don't have what it takes; we do."[3]

DONALD TRUMP

Donald J. Trump was born in Queens, New York, in 1946. He graduated from the Wharton School of the University of Pennsylvania with a degree in economics. He expanded his father's successful real estate business into an empire. In 2004, he gained national fame for starring in the reality show *The Apprentice*. Trump contemplated a run for the presidency several times but found little support. In 2015, he entered a crowded field for the Republican nomination. Trump, who had never held elected office, found burgeoning support among voters who felt the political system did not represent their interests. To the surprise of many political experts, Trump won the majority of votes during the Republican primary season. He accepted the party's nomination at the Republican National Convention in July 2016.

Clinton's speech did not dwell on the specifics of her intentions to increase jobs, reform the criminal justice system, and combat climate change. Instead, she elaborated on the mantra for the evening and the entire convention: unity. Delegates held signs that stated: "Stronger Together." Hillary echoed this slogan. "Let's be stronger together, my fellow Americans. Let's look to the future with courage and confidence. Let's build a better tomorrow for our beloved children and our beloved country. . . ."[4] Hundreds of red, white, and blue balloons dropped from the ceiling as the convention ended. If history was any judge, Clinton was ready. Her life so far had proven Clinton was a fighter.

A DAUGHTER'S INTRODUCTION

Before Clinton took the stage to accept the nomination of the Democratic Party, Clinton's daughter, Chelsea, introduced her mother to the cheering crowd. Chelsea shared stories of her relationship with her mother and father, former president William "Bill" Clinton. Chelsea explained how the work Hillary Clinton did throughout her career shaped her mother's character. "She never, ever forgets who she's fighting for. . . . That's who my mom is. She's a listener and a doer. She's a woman driven by compassion, by faith, by a fierce sense of justice, and a heart full of love."[5] Hillary Clinton stepped onto the stage as Chelsea finished her introduction, a smile on her face and, momentarily, tears in her eyes.

CHAPTER
TWO

NO ROOM FOR COWARDS

Hillary Diane Rodham was born in Chicago, Illinois, on October 26, 1947, the first child of Hugh and Dorothy Rodham. Her younger brothers, Hugh and Tony, came along a few years later. In 1950, the family moved to the suburb of Park Ridge, Illinois. This middle-class, white, mostly Republican community helped mold young Hillary.

Politics is not for the faint of heart, and Hillary learned to be tough as a preschooler. A bigger girl named Suzy lived next door to Hillary and often picked on her. One day, when Hillary raced in the house to escape the bully, Hillary's mother said, "If Suzy hits you . . . hit her back. There's no room in this house for cowards."[1] Four-year-old Hillary squared her little shoulders and marched back outside. She confronted Suzy, and the two became friends. Hillary has been fighting battles ever since.

Hillary, the oldest of three siblings, grew up in a suburb of Chicago, Illinois.

The Odd Couple

Hillary's father, Hugh, was tight-lipped, sullen, and hardworking. He grew up in Scranton, Pennsylvania. During the Great Depression, Hugh hopped a train for Chicago, where he found a job as a drapery fabric salesman. At a textile company, Hugh caught the eye of a clerk, Dorothy Howell. They married in 1942.

Hugh enlisted in the military but remained in the United States throughout World War II (1939–1945), training recruits for the navy. He was well suited for the role of tough drill sergeant, as his children would later learn the hard way.

After the war, Hugh opened a drapery business and fabric print plant. Hugh was a conservative Republican who believed people should pull themselves up by their bootstraps. The less involved the government was in people's lives, the better. He worked hard and expected his children

TOUGH LOVE

For years, Hillary and her father could barely speak to each other without fighting. In 1993, he suffered a massive stroke and lay in a coma. Hillary spent hours by his bedside, contemplating their relationship. His lingering death helped her reach a place of acceptance. "I . . . understood that even when he erupted at me, he admired my independence and . . . loved me with all his heart," she remembered.[2]

to work hard as well. Sometimes Hillary and her brothers helped their father with large orders. But Hugh did not pay his children for the work. Instead, he drove them through Chicago's slums to show his kids how fortunate they were.

Hugh ran his home like a military boot camp, barking orders from his living room chair. After living through hardship during the Great Depression, he hated waste. No matter how cold the temperature, Hugh turned the heat off at night. If someone forgot to put the toothpaste cap back on, Hugh threw the tube out the window and the kids had to go hunt for it outside.

Hillary described her father as a "tough taskmaster."[3] He could also be unkind. Once she came home with a report card. She had earned all As except for one B. Hugh said her school was too easy. At the dinner table, he threw out topics for discussion as though challenging his family to a verbal duel. If his wife said something Hugh disagreed with, he called her "Miss Smarty Pants."[4]

Hillary's mother, Dorothy, had an iron grit that came from surviving a childhood of neglect. When she was eight, Dorothy's parents loaded her on a train with her little sister and sent them to California to live with their grandparents. Their grandmother was cruel. She once confined Dorothy to her bedroom for an entire year as punishment for going trick-or-treating, allowing her out only to attend school. At age 14, Dorothy took a job as a live-in nanny and escaped her grandparents' house. After high school graduation, she returned to Chicago, where she met Hugh.

Dorothy quietly endured marriage to a man who was often mean because she believed marriage was a lifelong commitment. However, she was not spineless. Despite Hugh's tendency to forcefully share his conservative opinions, Dorothy quietly voted Democratic. She believed the government had a role in helping disadvantaged people. She challenged her husband when it was in Hillary's best interest. For example, Dorothy allowed Hillary to attend a 1961 sermon by Dr. Martin Luther King Jr. although Hugh had forbidden it.

Dorothy taught her daughter that nothing should stand in the way of her dreams. Armed with this conviction, 14-year-old Hillary set her sights on space. She wrote a letter to NASA, volunteering her services as an astronaut. Their reply was blunt: girls were not accepted in the astronaut training program. Hillary realized that though what her mother said was true,

Hillary was a smart student who was active in lots of school activities.

it would take hard work to remove what seemed like insurmountable obstacles.

A Political Education

Hillary loved school and worked hard to earn top grades. In elementary school, she was labeled the teacher's pet. In high school, hours of study, a good memory, and a keen sense of competition kept Hillary on the honor roll. She graduated in 1965 as a National Merit Scholar finalist.

Leadership and service came naturally to Hillary. She participated in cookie sales for the Girl Scouts

In high school, Hillary was a natural leader who was interested in politics.

and organized mock Olympics for the United Way.
At school, she was involved in yearbook, student
government, the high school newspaper, and the
academic quiz bowl.

Hillary exuded confidence. Dorothy had nurtured
this trait, telling her daughter, "You're unique. You can
think for yourself."[5] Classmate Art Curtis remembered
the first time he met Hillary. It was 1960, and she

chatted about Barry Goldwater, the conservative senator from Arizona. As a young student, Hillary had adopted her father's conservative political views. While other girls at school discussed boys and makeup, Curtis remembers Hillary as "absolutely political when politics wasn't cool."[6]

For Hillary, politics was not just about making speeches. It was about taking action. After Democrat John F. Kennedy defeated Republican Richard Nixon in the 1960 presidential election, Hillary and a friend hopped a bus to downtown Chicago to root out voter fraud. Neither girl had told her parents of their plans. Hillary boldly knocked on doors and asked people their

GOLDWATER GIRL

Barry Goldwater was a conservative senator from Arizona who ran for president in 1964. Hillary's freshman social studies teacher gave her a copy of Goldwater's book, *The Conscience of a Conservative*. It laid out the senator's rationale for a limited role for the federal government. Intrigued, Hillary wrote a 75-page paper on the conservative movement. She admired the senator and became a Goldwater Girl.

These young women dressed in cowgirl outfits and straw hats and worked on the senator's campaign. After Goldwater's loss in the 1964 presidential election, Hillary went into Chicago's minority neighborhoods to check for voter fraud. When she saw how grinding poverty restricted opportunities for African Americans, her view about the role of government in improving people's lives began changing.

names so she could match them to a voter list. One address turned out to be a tavern. Undaunted, Hillary marched inside and asked the men at the bar if anyone lived there. She was ordered out.

Hillary had assumed her father, a Nixon supporter, would be proud of her work for the Republican Party. Instead, he was furious when he found out she had been wandering the rough neighborhoods of Chicago's South Side.

In her senior year in high school, Hillary entered politics. Her Maine East High was overcrowded, so Hillary and half her classmates were transferred to Maine South for their final year. In this new environment, she ran against several boys for student body president. Hillary was defeated by a landslide. She had not expected to win, but the loss "still hurt, especially because one of my opponents said I was 'really stupid if I thought a girl could be elected president.'"[7]

Fueled by Faith

Rodham family life was centered on the First United Methodist Church of Park Ridge. Hillary attended Sunday school, Bible school, and youth group. She said her family "talked with God, walked with God, ate,

studied and argued with God."[8]
Hillary believed in the guiding
principle of John Wesley, the
founder of Methodism: "Do
all the good you can, by all the
means you can, in all the ways
you can, in all the places you
can, at all the times you can, to
all the people you can, as long as
ever you can."[9]

When Hillary was 14,
Don Jones became her youth
minister. He taught her how
to put John Wesley's principle
into action. Jones strove to open
teenagers' minds to the world outside Park Ridge. He
brought in an atheist speaker to debate a Christian one,
and a Jewish rabbi to discuss Judaism. The teens read
controversial literature, studied bold art, and listened to
the messages in rock-and-roll music. Armed with these
experience, Hillary was ready for the next step on her
journey: college.

COURAGE . . . AND A FIRST DATE

Hillary's best friend tried to set up her with a boy named Jim for the senior prom. Jim thought Hillary was nerdy but agreed to take her on a date. He drove to the top of a long hill, took out his skateboard, and asked Hillary if she had ever ridden one before. She had not, but she refused to admit it. Undaunted, she skateboarded down the hill without falling. Impressed, Jim took Hillary to the senior prom.

CHAPTER THREE

THE MAKING OF AN ACTIVIST

In the fall of 1965, Hillary Rodham arrived at Wellesley College, a women's college in Wellesley, Massachusetts. She remembers beginning college with her "father's political beliefs and . . . mother's dreams."[1] Both were destined to change.

Personal and Political Transformation

At first, Rodham did not like college. She recalled she "felt lonely, overwhelmed and out of place."[2] Although she eventually made friends, she still struggled periodically. Rodham fretted that she felt disconnected from the goals and dreams of other middle-class Americans.

While Rodham was at Wellesley, the feminist movement of the 1960s was blossoming. She began finding her voice. The all-female campus provided what she called "psychic space" where she could focus

At Wellesley College, Rodham earned a reputation as a smart, politically active student.

on learning rather than her appearance or men. Rodham had arrived on campus with her Republican views mostly intact. Freshmen year she was elected president of the Young Republicans Club. However, campus life bombarded her with experiences she had never known growing up in Park Ridge. Her political views shifted. When Rodham realized she was out of sync with the mainstream views of the Republican Party, she resigned as club president.

The civil rights movement hastened Rodham's political transformation. Before college, the only African Americans she knew were those who worked for her father. Now she had African-American classmates and friends engaged in protests to gain their full rights as American citizens. Rodham admitted feeling self-conscious as these friendships developed and "hyperaware" that she was moving further away from her father's values.[3]

The assassination of Dr. Martin Luther King Jr. in 1968 provoked Rodham to take action on her new political values. King's murder enraged her. Upon hearing the news, she threw her backpack against the wall and yelled, "I can't stand it anymore!"[4] The following day, she joined a protest march through Boston, Massachusetts.

Wellesley students had been demanding that the college recruit more African-American faculty and students. Their cries for change grew louder after King's death. Some students wanted to go on strike and close down the campus until their demands were met. Rodham was more interested in tangible change. She had just been elected student body president. In this role, Rodham mediated between angry students and the slow-to-change administration. Her leadership yielded results. The college developed strategies to increase campus diversity.

PRESIDENT RODHAM

Rodham was elected president of Wellesley's student government in 1968. She campaigned door-to-door in every dorm for weeks. When she found out she had won, Rodham was elated. She repeatedly told one professor, "I can't believe what just happened!"[5] She lobbied to change the curriculum and reform some of the school's strict social rules.

Rodham spent the summer of 1968 working for congressional leadership on Capitol Hill.

The 1968 Presidential Race

The Vietnam War (1955–1975) also divided the nation. By 1968, more than 500 American soldiers were dying each month in the war in Southeast Asia.[6] Although she had not completely abandoned the Republican Party, Rodham campaigned for Senator Eugene McCarthy, an antiwar Democrat who was running for president in 1968. She stuffed envelopes and knocked on doors for him. McCarthy ultimately lost the Democratic primary to the more moderate Hubert Humphrey.

That summer, Rodham received an internship to work with two Republican congressmen, Melvin Laird and Charles Goodell. Goodell sent Rodham to the Republican National Convention in Florida. This experience provided a "first inside look at big-time politics," she recalled.[7] When convention delegates nominated Richard Nixon as their presidential candidate, Rodham knew the Republican Party was too conservative for her. She wrote later, "I didn't leave the Republican Party as much as it left me."[8]

Rodham returned home to Illinois in time for the Democratic National Convention in Chicago. Thousands of protesters outside the convention hall demanded a swift end to the Vietnam War. Rodham and a friend headed downtown to watch. When they reached Grant Park, they smelled tear gas and saw the blue line of police. Someone in the crowd threw a rock, just missing Rodham. As the police charged the protestors, Rodham and her friend scrambled for safety.

The chaos of 1968 troubled her, but Rodham still believed political action was the only way to achieve long-lasting change. Although uncertain about what career she wanted, Rodham was determined to work in some capacity to improve the lives of others.

Rodham began raising her voice for social justice even before she finished her degree at Wellesley.

Graduating from Wellesley

During her senior year at Wellesley, from 1968–1969, Rodham wrote her thesis on the community organizer Saul Alinsky. He believed poor people needed to be empowered. He argued that unjust institutions could be changed only by efforts made by people outside those institutions. Rodham agreed that endowing the underprivileged with a strong voice was vital. But she believed a capable leader could work inside the system to improve society. This made her decide to go to law school and work for justice.

Wellesley had never had a student speaker at graduation—until Hillary Rodham came along. Some students threatened to protest during the ceremony if their student body president was not allowed to address the crowd. The college administrator relented.

Senator Edward Brooke of Massachusetts spoke before Rodham. He was the highest-ranking African-American politician in the country, and the only African American in the US Senate. In his speech, he empathized with the goals of the student protests but condemned their actions. Although Rodham had campaigned for Brooke, she was disappointed by his tepid speech. When her turn to speak came, she went off script. "Empathy doesn't do us anything," she railed. "The challenge now is to practice politics as the art of making what appears to be impossible, possible."[9]

Rodham's speech got a mixed reaction. College officials

FISH SLIMING

The summer after graduating from Wellesley, Rodham worked in Alaska cleaning fish in a salmon factory. She wore knee-high boots and stood in water while she slimed out salmon guts with a spoon. One day Rodham told a supervisor the fish looked rotten. He fired her on the spot. When she returned the next day to pick up her check, the entire operation had been packed up. She later said sliming fish in Alaska "was pretty good preparation for life in Washington."[10]

were angry and embarrassed that she had targeted Brooke. But people outside campus were intrigued. *Life* magazine featured Rodham, and reporters called her for interviews. Armed with a bachelor's degree in political science, Hillary left Wellesley in 1969 and headed to law school.

GENDER BARRIERS

Rodham was accepted to both Harvard and Yale law schools and could not decide which one to attend. A male friend invited her to a cocktail party at Harvard, where he introduced her to a well-known law professor. The friend said Rodham was having a hard time deciding if she should come to Harvard or "sign up with our closest competitor." The professor gave Rodham a long look and said, "First of all, we don't have any close competitors. Secondly, we don't need any more women at Harvard."[12] Rodham picked Yale.

Legal Training

While Rodham was at Yale Law School, the Vietnam War continued to be a political and social concern on college campuses. On May 4, 1970, the National Guard fired on student protesters at Kent State University in Ohio, killing four students. When Rodham heard the news, she ran out of her classroom in tears.

Despite her grief, Rodham took the lead. She moderated a passionate debate among her classmates over what stance they should take in the wake of these deaths. One classmate described her as a sort of "translator."[11] With her leadership, students felt heard and understood. They voted overwhelmingly to join 300 other schools on a national strike.

In the summer of 1970, Rodham moved to Washington to work for Marian Wright Edelman's Washington Research Project. Edelman was a former civil rights organizer and the first black woman admitted to the bar in Mississippi. For four weeks, Rodham compiled information on the conditions of migrant workers' families for a Senate investigation. As a teenager, she had babysat the children of migrant workers in Illinois and seen the difficulties migrant families faced up close. Now she was working to help them. This summer marked a turning point in her life.

The future suddenly seemed clear. When she returned to school, Rodham created her own study program. She took a combination of law, medicine, and psychology classes to understand child development. She helped the Yale–New Haven hospital create legal procedures for cases of suspected child abuse. Rodham explained that she wanted to use the law "to give voice to children who were not being heard."[13] But then something interrupted her plans. She fell in love.

CHAPTER FOUR

LOVE AND POLITICS

Bill Clinton was sitting in class at Yale Law School when his gaze fell on a student he had not noticed before. "She had thick dark blond hair and wore eyeglasses and no makeup, but she conveyed a sense of strength and self-possession I had rarely seen in anyone, man or woman," Bill recalled.[1] The student was Hillary Rodham. Intrigued, Bill began following her around campus. When Rodham noticed the tall, burly man with a big beard, she thought he looked "more like a Viking than a . . . scholar."[2] Eventually, she agreed to go on a date with him. Before long, they were a couple.

Sacrifices

Rodham was on track to graduate in 1972, but Bill still had another year of classes. She decided to postpone her graduation. That summer she worked once again for Marian Wright Edelman, who by this time had founded the Children's Defense Fund. Rodham investigated private schools that refused to admit students of color.

Rodham first introduced herself to Bill in the law library at Yale.

Schools that discriminated were not supposed to get tax breaks. But the federal government was not enforcing this law. In Alabama, Rodham posed as a mother interested in enrolling her child in school, and one principal promised "no black students would be enrolled."[3] With the evidence Rodham gathered, the Defense Fund pressured the federal government to apply existing law.

Later that summer, Rodham joined Bill in Texas, where he was in charge of the get-out-the-vote effort for George McGovern's presidential campaign. Rodham was based in San Antonio and roomed with Sara Ehrman, a

BILL'S BACKGROUND

William Jefferson Clinton was born in Hope, Arkansas, in 1946. His father died a few months before he was born, and his mother later married an abusive alcoholic. Despite this chaotic childhood, Bill excelled at school. In 1963, he went to Washington, DC, as part of Boy's Nation, an American Legion program. While there, he met President John F. Kennedy.

After graduating from high school in 1964, Bill attended Georgetown University. Personable, attractive, and charismatic, he was elected president of his freshman and sophomore classes. He won a prestigious Rhodes scholarship to study at Oxford in England, although he never completed a degree there. Bill returned to the United States in 1970 and enrolled in Yale Law School, where he met Rodham. But politics, not law, was Bill's passion. He would serve one term as Arkansas's attorney general, five terms as governor of Arkansas, and two terms as president of the United States.

veteran political organizer. Ehrman nicknamed Rodham "Fearless" because she was unafraid to knock on doors in tough neighborhoods.[4] Betsy Wright, a Texas native, also worked with Rodham and was "obsessed with how far Hillary might go, with her mixture of brilliance, ambition, and self-assuredness."[5] Wright was convinced Rodham could be the nation's first female president.

Both Rodham and Bill graduated from Yale Law School in 1973 and celebrated by taking a trip to England. One evening, as they sat on the shores of Lake Ennerdale, Bill proposed. Rodham said no. Although she loved him, Rodham knew Bill planned to return to Arkansas and run for office. She was not ready to commit to a future in that state.

Fighting for Children

Bill moved to Fayetteville to teach at the University of Arkansas School of Law, and Rodham settled in Cambridge, Massachusetts, as a staff attorney for the Children's Defense Fund. She was pursuing her dream of becoming an advocate for children.

Rodham's job was to investigate cases where children's rights were being violated. She inspected jails in South Carolina, where teens convicted of minor offenses were housed with hardened adult criminals. She knocked on doors in Massachusetts to track down truant students only to discover they were babysitting handicapped siblings unable to attend school because of a disability. The Children's Defense Fund used data from Rodham's investigations to pressure state legislatures and Congress for reforms.

Investigating Nixon

Although she was passionate about children's issues, an opportunity came along in January 1974 that Rodham could not pass up. House and Senate committees were examining whether President Richard Nixon had tried to cover up a 1972 burglary of the Democratic Party's headquarters in the Watergate Hotel. John Doar, the chief lawyer for the House Judiciary Committee, asked Rodham to join his team of lawyers investigating the case. If they could prove Nixon had committed a crime, Nixon would be impeached and removed from office.

Through the spring and summer of 1974, Rodham and 43 other attorneys worked 12 to 16 hours a day, seven days a week. Rodham researched historical cases of impeachment to determine what acts were impeachable offenses. She and her team did not have

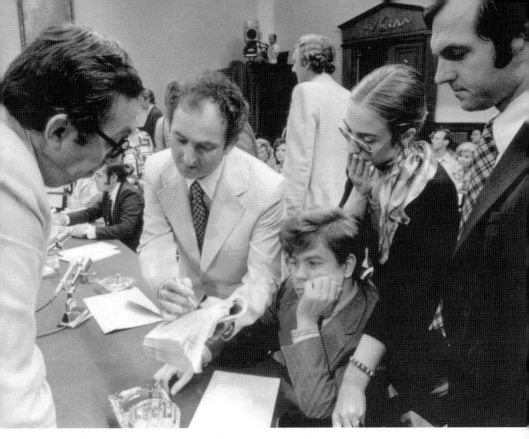

Rodham worked with the legal team that compiled evidence that Nixon broke the law while running for president.

computers to help them. The legal team compiled 500,000 index cards of facts to build a convincing case that Nixon had broken the law. Ultimately, Nixon resigned on August 9, 1974, before he could be tried.

This experience was sobering for Rodham. She believed the impeachment process had forced a corrupt president out of office and "was a victory for the Constitution."[6] But she also saw the immense power of congressional committees. She concluded the impeachment system was only as "fair and just and constitutional as the men and women" who led the committees.[7]

After Nixon resigned, Rodham was out of work. She could have had her pick of jobs in Washington, but she was ready to follow her heart. She missed Bill. She decided to give Arkansas a chance.

Moving to Arkansas

With a vibrant university, barbecue feasts, and the Razorback football team, Fayetteville, Arkansas, was not the backwoods Rodham had feared. She joined Bill as a faculty member at the University of Arkansas School of Law. She quickly earned a reputation as a tough, but fair, professor. One former student said Rodham would "rip you pretty good" if you were not prepared for class.[8] But she did not try to humiliate students, only challenged them to think more deeply.

Rodham also ran the university's legal aid clinic and a prisoner assistance project. In the spring of 1975, she was assigned a case in which she had to defend a factory worker accused of raping a 12-year-old girl. She defended her client vigorously, even questioning the girl's credibility, which was a standard practice in rape cases. She worked out a plea bargain for her client. But the case had troubled her, and when it ended, Rodham created Arkansas's first rape crisis hotline.

Bill Runs for Office

Bill decided to run for Congress in 1974. A victory would mean he would be based in Washington, DC, much of the year, and Rodham could pursue her dreams there without living apart from him.

Rodham gave Bill campaign advice almost daily. Although he had never run for office before, he had enemies. Some people considered him an outsider because he had lived out of state for a time. Others opposed his northern girlfriend. Rumors were spread that he was both gay and living with Rodham outside of

MAKE YOUR OWN COFFEE

The female lawyers working on the Nixon case were exposed to not-so-subtle sexism from their male colleagues. In response, Rodham and the other women in the office posted a sign on the coffee machine that stated: "The women in this office were not hired to make coffee." It directed the men to either make it themselves or ask one of their male colleagues to do the job.

marriage, although they did not live together.

Ultimately, Bill lost the election by just 6,000 votes.[9] This was actually good news. His opponent had been a four-term incumbent and had won by only two percentage points. Everyone knew Bill would run for office in Arkansas again in 1976. Rodham realized her dream of returning to Washington with Bill was not going to happen anytime soon. She had a decision to make.

Wedding Bells

In the fall of 1975, Rodham traveled north for some soul-searching. Bill drove her to the airport, and on the way they passed a red-brick house that was for sale. Rodham mentioned that she liked it. Then off she flew for Boston, New York, Washington, DC, and Chicago. As she traveled, she weighed the pros and cons of life in the north versus life in Arkansas. Somewhere along the way, she made up her mind.

When Bill picked Rodham up at the airport, he casually asked if she remembered the little red-brick house. She did. "Well, I bought it," he said, "so now you'd better marry me because I can't live in it by myself."[10] This time, she said yes.

The couple was married in the front room of their new home on October 11, 1975. Rodham stunned the wedding crowd when she announced she would keep her maiden name. Bill's mother cried at the news, and his campaign manager cringed, afraid of the political consequences. Even the newspapers commented on her decision. Rodham told a friend her name was part of her identity and helped ensure that she was "a person in my own right."[11] Rodham never dreamed such a simple and private decision would have such dramatic and public consequences.

CHAPTER
FIVE

POLITICAL BATTLES IN THE RAZORBACK STATE

Rodham faced a dilemma. She wanted to advocate for children, but pay in the nonprofit world was low. Bill was elected Arkansas attorney general in 1976, but he did not make much money as a public official. When they moved to Little Rock for Bill's new job, Rodham realized she needed to safeguard the family's financial future.

First Female Lawyer

Vince Foster was a childhood friend of Bill's and a lawyer with the Rose Law Firm, a prestigious company that practiced corporate law. Foster recommended Rodham to his partners, and she was hired as the firm's first female lawyer.

The newlyweds were ready to take Arkansas politics by storm.

It was a difficult transition. Rodham was not afraid to speak her mind and was not intimidated by anyone. Some people were put off by her confidence. However, Rodham became fast friends with Foster and Webb Hubbell, another of the firm's lawyers. The trio called themselves the "Three Amigos."[1]

The first jury trial Rodham handled on her own was the defense of a canning company. A man who had found a rat's hindquarters in a can of pork and beans sued the company. He claimed the sight had so disgusted him that he could not stop spitting, and consequently, could not kiss his fiancée. Rodham mounted a solid defense, and her work resulted in her client paying a tiny award. But she was very nervous before the jury. Thereafter,

SEXISM IN THE WORKPLACE

Her passion for politics forced Rodham into a world traditionally inhabited by men. One evening in 1976, Rodham was having dinner in Indiana with a group of volunteers. They had all spent the day campaigning for the presidential candidate, Governor Jimmy Carter. Rodham, the only woman present, pressured the men for details on how many phone calls they had made and how many doors they had knocked on. Suddenly, one man lunged across the table and grabbed her by the shirt. "Just shut up, will you," he yelled. "We said we'd do it . . . and we don't have to tell you how!" Rodham kept her cool. "First," she said, "don't ever touch me again. Second, if you were as fast with the answers to my questions as you are with your hands, I'd have the information I need to do my job."[2]

she mainly did legal work that did not require arguing in court.

First Lady of Arkansas

In 1978, Bill ran for governor of Arkansas. Rodham played only a minor role in the campaign, but this did not protect her from being targeted by Republican opponents. Bill was criticized for having a wife with a career. A newspaper columnist wrote that even Bill's wife did not like him enough to take his last name. The image Bill's opponents painted about Rodham reached the entire nation. After Bill won the election, the *New York Times* newspaper reported that he was "married to an ardent feminist."[3] To conservatives, this was not a compliment.

Rodham continued working for the Rose Law Firm while acting as unofficial adviser to her husband. People expected her to be a traditional First Lady. But she did not attend ladies' luncheons, a traditional function of a governor's wife. She had no interest in standing silent and smiling alongside her husband. One columnist wrote that Rodham "just went her own way. . . . A lot of people thought she was remote, distant."[4] Rodham did not read the newspapers or watch news coverage about

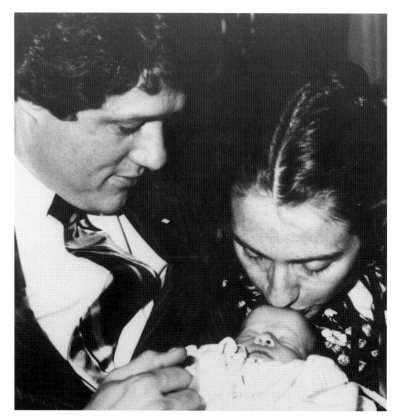

Rodham and Bill welcomed daughter Chelsea after Bill lost reelection.

her. It was not worth stressing over things she could not change. As a result, she was ignorant of the public's growing negative perception of her.

Early in his term, Bill signed a bill to increase car licensing fees. His goal was to raise much-needed revenue, but the law was very unpopular. Then a reporter broke the story that Rodham had not paid taxes on her automobile for the previous two years.

She owed only $79 in back taxes.[5] But she had gotten new license plates without paying the tax, giving people the impression that she and the governor thought they were above the law.

Bill was decisively defeated in his 1980 bid for reelection. He was devastated and fell into a deep depression. Rodham knew he needed to recover politically if he was going to recover emotionally. Shortly after the election, she told his campaign manager to begin planning his next run for office. Then she set about reshaping her image.

In the fall of 1981, Bill's political resurrection began with Rodham in charge. First, she insisted Bill apologize to the people of Arkansas. When he hesitated, she said, "Put aside your damned pride and show them that you get it."[6] He did.

Then Rodham changed her name. Bill did not pressure her, saying her name was

IT'S A GIRL!

In early 1980, the couple was eagerly awaiting the birth of their first child. When Rodham went into labor early, Bill ran about grabbing things to take to the hospital. He yelled at a state trooper to get a bag of ice. The couple's birthing class recommended Rodham suck on ice chips during labor. Rodham watched as the trooper tossed a 39-gallon (148 kg) bag of ice into the trunk. She wound up having a cesarean section and did not need any ice, let alone 39 gallons worth. On February 27, 1980, Chelsea Victoria Clinton was born.

her business. But Rodham decided "it was more important for Bill to be governor again than for me to keep my maiden name."[7] Hillary Clinton plunged into campaigning with gusto. The press called her the best speaker of all the politicians' wives. Her strategy worked. Bill was reelected with 55 percent of the vote.[8]

Fighting for Education Reform

Education reform became Clinton's pet project during her husband's second term. He appointed her chairperson of the Governor's Education Standards Committee. At the time, Arkansas had the highest percentage of American students who failed achievement tests and the lowest percentage of American students who attended college. Clinton knew educational reform would be politically risky. Any meaningful reform meant raising taxes on Arkansans.

To gain support for her reforms, Clinton targeted teacher performance. She fought for reforms that would require testing for teachers. It was a bitter debate. One school librarian called Clinton "lower than a snake's belly."[9] Clinton wore their animosity as a badge of honor, convinced results would someday prove her right.

The Arkansas educational system did improve during Bill's five terms as governor. But reforms came at the cost of the support of the state's teachers. Still, Clinton believed she had developed a successful model for reforming large institutions.

Run for the White House

On October 3, 1991, Clinton dusted off her campaign skills when Bill announced he was running for president. He defeated his Democratic opponents and secured the party's nomination. George H. W. Bush was the Republican president seeking reelection. The Bush campaign launched an unceasing attack against both Clintons. Bill was characterized as a draft dodger and even a sexual predator and murderer. The national press reported on allegations of Bill's sexual affairs with

HOLDING BACK

As Bill's poll numbers dipped during the 1992 presidential election campaign, consultants tinkered with Clinton's image. She stopped speaking at events. Instead, she smiled and remained silent at Bill's side, even holding an umbrella over his head when it rained. The press poked fun at the idea that she was keeping a low profile. Near the end of the campaign, a newspaper cartoon showed Bill speaking into a human-sized box with air holes, saying, "Only a few days more, Hillary."[10]

women in Arkansas. Clinton was labeled as a radically progressive, lesbian feminist.

Clinton faced the allegations head-on. She hired a team to defuse negative stories before they gained traction. She and Bill appeared on the television program *60 Minutes* to discuss their commitment to their marriage. One aide said Clinton viewed her life as "a series of battles. . . . She's happiest when she's fighting."[11]

As the campaign progressed, Clinton's image suffered. While trying to explain the difficult choices working mothers faced, she made a statement that came back to bite her. "I suppose I could have stayed home," she said, "baked cookies, and had teas."[12] She had made the statement in response to an allegation that as governor, her husband had improperly helped her career as an attorney. But the full context of her statement was not reported. The campaign received many angry phone calls from professional women who had taken time off to raise their children.

Bill had been campaigning with the motto "Buy one, get one free."[13] If he was elected, he reasoned, the nation would also get a highly skilled First Lady. Suddenly, that strategy did not seem wise. Republicans described

The Clintons celebrate Bill's nomination for president.

Clinton as both a radical feminist and an intolerable
wife. So the Democrats changed tactics. Clinton stopped
speaking at events and even won a cookie bake-off
against First Lady Barbara Bush.

These changes to Clinton's public image seemed to
work. Bill won the 1992 election. When the results
came in, thousands of people crowded the Arkansas
State House, sounding the cheer of the Razorback
football team. The couple from Arkansas was headed to
Washington, DC.

CHAPTER
SIX

WHITE HOUSE WORK

C rowds thronged Pennsylvania Avenue on
January 20, 1993, for Bill's presidential
inauguration. Shrieks of "We want Hillary!" could be
heard through the bulletproof glass of the presidential
limousine.[1] The first family walked the last blocks of the
parade route, Clinton striding confidently a few yards
ahead of her husband. It was the first day of her new job.
But as Clinton later wrote, "There is no training manual
for First Ladies."[2] She would learn on the job, often the
hard way.

Hillaryland

The White House has two wings. Traditionally, First
Ladies operate out of the East Wing, which contains
offices, a reception area, a movie theater, and a glass
corridor overlooking the Rose Garden. The West Wing
holds the Oval Office, Cabinet Room, and Situation

Bill and Hillary Clinton wave to the crowd on Inauguration Day,
January 20, 1993.

Room. But Clinton wanted an office where the power lay—in the West Wing.

A corner office on the second floor of the West Wing and a suite in the Old Executive Office Building housed Clinton and her staff of 20 men and women. These spaces became known as Hillaryland. Close proximity to the Oval Office gave her stature and access to the president. While she and Bill both believed this was deserved, it worried other members of the administration. Top aides feared Clinton's closeness to the president would spark fears he was the First Lady's puppet.

CONVERSATIONS WITH ELEANOR

First Lady Eleanor Roosevelt is Clinton's hero. Clinton collects pictures and mementos of the former First Lady's life. The wife of President Franklin Delano Roosevelt shared Clinton's values about child welfare and civil and human rights. First Lady Roosevelt also faced scathing criticism because she cared more about public policy than being a traditional politician's wife. As First Lady, Clinton followed a trail that Roosevelt had blazed through poor rural and urban neighborhoods and far-off foreign cities. In difficult times, Clinton carries on imaginary conversations with Roosevelt, finding comfort in lines like this one: "A woman is like a teabag. You never know how strong she is until she's in hot water."[3] When Clinton was downcast following Democratic defeats in the 1994 congressional election, she wondered what Roosevelt would think of her situation. "Not much," Clinton concluded.[4] There was nothing to do but carry on.

Avoiding the Press

Clinton arrived in Washington leery of the press corps, embittered by how reporters had focused on scandals rather than issues during her husband's campaign. Clinton also believed Washington correspondents had an overly cozy relationship with government officials. She acted to change this.

White House reporters worked from cramped cubicles in the basement but could access government officials through a corridor that led to the West Wing. Clinton ordered this entrance blocked. Although the corridor was eventually reopened, the damage had been done. Usually when a new administration takes office, the press gives it a brief honeymoon before asking tough questions. Instead of a honeymoon, the press hammered the Clintons.

Health-Care Reform

In the campaign, Bill had pledged to pass affordable, quality health care for all Americans. With Clinton's enthusiastic consent, he appointed her to lead the President's Task Force on National Health Care Reform. This group was charged with overhauling the nation's

Clinton meets with a doctor's group in Chicago as the head of the Task Force on National Health Care Reform.

health-care system. The president vowed the task force would have a plan to present to Congress in the first 100 days of his administration.

In 1993, more than 37 million Americans were uninsured.[5] The cost of medical care was skyrocketing while the quality of care declined. The need for change was great, but reform required getting Congress, employers, the medical establishment, and insurance companies to reach an agreement. A massive undertaking like this would take months, even years. One hundred days was unrealistic.

Undaunted, Clinton tackled the health-care system and almost immediately ran into trouble. She tried to keep the identities of the 600 people working on planning committees a secret. She wanted these officials to work without the scrutiny of the press and pressure from lobbyists. However, the public viewed her motives differently, wondering what she had to hide. A group of doctors filed a successful lawsuit to get access to the names of the committee members.

Leaders of the Democratic Party felt alienated by Clinton's resistance to compromise. In April 1993, she met with top Democrats to update them on the progress of the reform bill. When some of them offered changes to her plan or suggested she slow down rather than rush to meet the 100-day deadline, Clinton balked. She said the White House would go after any member of Congress who obstructed their reforms. Senator Bill Bradley of New Jersey said, "That [meeting] was it for me in terms of Hillary Clinton. . . . The assumption that people with questions are enemies. The disdain. The hypocrisy."[6] Without the support of Democrats, a health-care reform bill could not pass. The 100-day deadline passed, but Clinton soldiered on. In the fall of 1993, she testified before House and Senate committees about her proposals. Even opponents were impressed with her command of the complex details of the health-care system. When the bill itself was finally presented to Congress on October 27, 1993, it was 1,342 pages long.[7] Few people could understand it.

After months of hard work and political wrangling, the health-care reform bill died a quiet death. The bill never even made it to the floor of the Senate for a vote. Despite this huge blow, Clinton did not give up the fight. Although she was not an elected official, she still worked with legislators to create the State Children's Health Insurance Program (S-CHIP) in 1997. Today this program provides medical insurance to more than eight million low- and moderate-income children.[8]

Travelgate and Heartbreak

Bill had pledged to end dishonesty and cronyism in his administration. However, the first time the Clintons tried to root out corruption, their efforts seriously backfired. The job of the White House Travel Office is to make travel arrangements for government officials and the press corps who accompany them. When Clinton heard allegations of corruption in this office, she repeatedly told aides to deal with the problem. On May 19, 1993, seven Travel Office employees were fired without warning. Because reporters had a good relationship with these people, White House correspondents were furious. When they reported the Clintons had filled the vacant jobs with friends and relatives, the couple was accused of cronyism.

This scandal, known as Travelgate, implicated Clinton because her aides had ordered the firings. She denied telling them to do so, and three investigations cleared her of any wrongdoing. Attention focused on the Clintons' friend Vince Foster, who was serving as the First Lady's top legal adviser.

INCOGNITO

On occasion, Clinton was desperate to escape the intense scrutiny of life in the White House. At those times, she donned sneakers, sunglasses, and a baseball cap and walked through the Washington Mall or rode her bike in Georgetown, a Secret Service member close by. One morning, a family asked her to snap its photograph in front of the Washington Monument. She graciously obliged. As she walked away, Clinton heard one of the kids say, "Mom, that lady looks familiar."[9]

Foster had not adjusted well to life in Washington. Travelgate pushed him to the breaking point. Afraid he would have to testify in a congressional investigation, Foster grew anxious and depressed. A *Wall Street Journal* editorial accused him of being careless about the law. On July 20, 1993, Foster shot himself. The news of her friend's death flattened Clinton. She was consumed by grief and guilt that she had not recognized the extent of his emotional crisis.

The FBI wanted to search Foster's apartment. Because he had confidential Clinton files in his home, one of the president's lawyers made FBI agents wait while he removed personal documents. These files were legally protected from law enforcement seizure because Foster's home was not a crime scene. The Justice Department classified Foster's death as a suicide.

Clinton Regroups

The cost of these political scandals hit home in the midterm elections of 1994. Republicans won control of both houses of Congress, and it was the first time since 1954 the party controlled the House of Representatives. The weeks after this election were some of Clinton's most difficult days as First Lady. She decided it was once again time to redefine her role.

Clinton withdrew from the national spotlight. She began writing the book *It Takes a Village* about the role a community plays in raising well-adjusted children. In March 1995, Clinton and 15-year-old Chelsea toured Asia. At schools, orphanages, and cultural functions, Clinton spoke eloquently on the importance of women's

Clinton visited a school for impoverished children in New Delhi, India, in 1995.

rights. American reporters who accompanied her began to view Clinton in a new light. They witnessed their First Lady's compassion, intelligence, and sense of humor.

In the summer of 1995, the United Nations' World Conference on Women was held in Beijing, China, a nation with which the United States had a fragile relationship. Clinton spoke before delegates from 180 nations, challenging them to address the violence and discrimination women faced across the world, including in China. "Human rights are women's rights, and women's rights are human rights," she declared to the assembly.[10] The audience gave her a standing ovation, although the Chinese government censored coverage of the speech. Her reputation rose at home. The *New York Times* lauded Clinton's speech as her best since becoming a public figure.

But another scandal developed during this time of public acclaim. This scandal threatened her family's very existence.

Special Counsel

On Halloween of 1993, a surprise waited for Clinton in the morning newspaper. The Clintons had entered into a land development agreement with their friends Jim and Susan McDougal in 1978. Together, the couples purchased 230 acres (93 ha) along the White River in Arkansas. They planned to subdivide the land, called Whitewater, and sell the lots for vacation homes. By the time the lots were ready for sale, the economy had tanked, and no one could afford vacation homes. The Clintons kept the land, letting Jim McDougal manage it. Now, this fateful decision had come back to haunt them.

Jim McDougal was under investigation for financial crimes. Prosecutors alleged McDougal had used money from his failed savings and loan company to funnel contributions to Bill's 1986 reelection campaign for

Clinton speaks with reporters about the Whitewater scandal on April 22, 1994.

governor, which was illegal. When the press picked up the story, they asked the Clintons for documents about the Whitewater deal. The Clintons ignored the requests. Soon reporters attempted to link the charges against McDougal with the files that had been removed from Foster's office after his suicide. Republican opponents began spreading rumors that the Clintons had ordered Foster murdered to cover up the Whitewater deal.

Republican leaders called for a special prosecutor, an independent investigator with extremely broad powers, to look into the deal. Clinton opposed such a move, but Bill was under pressure to clear up the matter. He believed they had done nothing illegal, so they might as well cooperate and put the rumors to rest. He authorized the appointment of a special prosecutor, Kenneth Starr. Later Bill said, "It was the worst presidential decision I ever made, wrong on the facts, wrong on the law, wrong on the politics, wrong for the presidency, and the Constitution."[11]

Stories about the Clintons' past exploded. When the Clintons could not produce certain financial documents in a timely manner, Starr suspected they were obstructing his investigation. In the winter of 1996, Clinton became the first First Lady to testify before a grand jury. The court determined there was insufficient evidence to charge her with any crime. But Starr had spent millions of taxpayer dollars investigating the Clintons, so Republicans pressured him to dig deeper. Starr shifted his attention to the president, requiring him to testify under oath about his relationship with a former White House intern named Monica Lewinsky. Starr suspected Bill had asked Lewinsky to lie to investigators about having an affair with him.

Bill had told Clinton that he had not had an affair with Lewinsky, and she believed him. She defended her husband repeatedly and publicly. Clinton told a friend, "My husband may have his faults, but he has never lied to me."[12] However, taped phone conversations and physical evidence unraveled Bill's story. On the morning of August 18, 1998, Bill woke his wife and told her he had lied to her. Clinton was devastated.

The Clinton marriage was in crisis. Clinton felt "nothing but profound sadness, disappointment and unresolved anger."[13] She could barely speak to Bill. Her former youth minister, Don Jones, reminded her that sin and grace exist in everyone simultaneously. As Clinton waited for grace, she carried on, one day at a time. Eventually, she was able to forgive her husband and help fight for his political future, and her own.

IMPEACHMENT

Political opponents seized on the Lewinsky scandal to try to destroy Bill Clinton's presidency. On December 19, 1998, the House of Representatives narrowly voted to impeach Clinton on charges of lying under oath and obstructing justice. Later that day, two busloads of Democratic members of Congress came to the White House to support the president. Hillary Clinton joined them, linking arms with her husband. Two months later, the Senate held Bill Clinton's impeachment trial. The Senate found the president not guilty on both counts.

CHAPTER SEVEN

PURSUIT OF DREAMS

In March 1999, Clinton went to the Lab School in Manhattan to promote a television special about women in sports. A huge banner in front of the stage displayed the words "Dare to Compete." When the captain of the school's girls' basketball team introduced Clinton, the girl whispered, "Dare to compete, Mrs. Clinton."[1]

For months, Democratic leaders had been pressuring Clinton to run for an open Senate seat from New York, though she did not live there. The state had loose residency requirements for its elected officials, but she still hesitated. Now the basketball player's remark made Clinton question whether she was afraid to take the kind of bold chance she had spent her life encouraging other women to take.

On February 6, 2000, Clinton formally announced her candidacy for senator of New York. She put a

First Lady Clinton set her sights on a New York senatorial seat in 2000.

positive spin on the charge that she was not a native New York. "I may be new to the neighborhood," she said, "but I am not new to your concerns."[2] Clinton vowed to focus on family issues such as health care and education. But political experts agreed Clinton had an uphill climb. Her main competitor, New York City mayor Rudy Giuliani, was a popular politician.

She made that climb. Giuliani dropped out of the race due to illness. With a decisive victory of 55 to 43 percent, Hillary Rodham Clinton was elected to the United States Senate on November 7, 2000.[3] She was the first First Lady to run for elective office and the first female US senator to represent the state of New York.

Senatorial Style

When Clinton took office on January 3, 2001, she was one of only 13 women in the Senate. For 17 days, she was also the only woman in history to simultaneously serve as First Lady and senator. Republican senators were determined to puncture any ego Clinton might bring to her new job. But Clinton kept her head down, listened closely, and worked hard. She served on the Budget Committee, the Committee on Health,

Education, Labor, and Pensions, and the Environment and Public Works Committee.

Clinton could be counted on to get things done for the citizens of New York. She did not hesitate to tackle the unglamorous work that improves a constituent's daily life. Clinton battled for funding for a section of New York interstate. She negotiated economic opportunities for farmers, wineries, and restaurant owners. She sponsored a bill to create a rating system for video games, though it did not pass.

But one event and its aftermath dominated Clinton's years in the Senate. On September 11, 2001, terrorists flew two planes into the Twin Towers of the World Trade Center in New York City. The towers collapsed, killing thousands of people. After the attack, Clinton and Charles

WORKHORSE

Colleagues in the Senate viewed Clinton as a hard worker and easy to get along with. Republican senator from Virginia John Warner said Clinton "did her homework, and she was well-prepared."[4] A Democratic senator called her "a workhorse, not a show horse."[5] She joined a Wednesday morning prayer group that included some conservative Republicans who had shot political barbs at her for many years. Working and praying together helped these former enemies see each other in a new light. Kansas senator Sam Brownback asked Clinton for forgiveness for the things he had said about her in the past. She willingly gave it.

Schumer, the senior senator from New York, lobbied Washington to provide money and services to crippled New York. Clinton fought for funding to monitor the air quality around Ground Zero, the hole where the World Trade Center towers had once stood. Congress pledged $20 billion but followed through with only $11 billion.[6] New Yorkers were upset. When Clinton went on stage at a benefit concert in October 2001, the crowd booed her. She shrugged it off, saying, "They can blow off steam any way they want to," and continued fighting for more aid.[7] She helped create the 9/11 Victims Compensation Fund and the 9/11 Commission that investigated the security flaws that led to the terrorist assault.

9/11

The sky was a robin's egg blue and the sun shone brilliantly on September 11, 2001. With horrifying swiftness, the beautiful morning turned into a nightmare when 19 terrorists commandeered four commercial jets. The hijackers deliberately crashed two planes into the World Trade Center in New York City. The third struck the Pentagon in Virginia, and the fourth plane crashed in a field in Pennsylvania. Almost 3,000 people died in the deadliest terrorist attack on American soil. The day after the attack, Clinton flew in a helicopter over Ground Zero in New York City. Smoke was still rising from the twisted girders and shattered beams.

Hillary and the Iraq War

President George W. Bush identified the terrorist organization al-Qaeda as the perpetrator of the 9/11 attacks. The Taliban government of Afghanistan was sheltering Osama bin Laden, the leader of al-Qaeda. Clinton joined the majority of Congress in signing a resolution authorizing President Bush to use force against al-Qaeda and all who aided them. In October, the United States went to war in Afghanistan.

In 2003, Clinton gained a seat on the Armed Services Committee. She asked defense experts to tutor her on military strategy and the financial complexities of weapon and equipment purchases. She never missed a committee meeting and sometimes was the sole senator in the chamber questioning military experts.

When the hunt for bin Laden stalled, President Bush shifted his attention to Iraq, a nation governed by dictator Saddam Hussein. In the fall of 2002, Bush accused Hussein of building weapons of mass destruction and harboring terrorists. When Hussein did not comply with international inspections of Iraqi weapons development facilities, Bush pressured

Congress for the authority to use force to topple the Iraqi leader.

Prior to the Senate's vote on Bush's request, Clinton did her homework. She studied briefings from experts and reviewed reports from weapons inspectors. She asked Bush officials tough questions about their postinvasion plans, concerned about a potential power vacuum in the Middle East if Hussein was removed.

On October 10, 2002, Clinton took the Senate floor to voice her tentative approval for the use of military force in Iraq. She believed President Bush was committed to working with the United Nations to get Saddam Hussein to comply through negotiations rather than force. She sincerely believed the president would do everything he could to avoid going to war. Clinton acknowledged that voting to send American soldiers into harm's way was "probably the hardest decision I have ever had to make."[8] But her tendency to endorse war earned her the nickname Hillary the Hawk among the press. The authorization passed on a vote of 77 to 23.[9] In March 2003, the United States went to war in Iraq.

As a senator, Clinton had limited power to impact how the wars in Afghanistan and Iraq were fought.

Clinton visited troops in Iraq and Afghanistan in 2003 after voting in favor of war in Iraq.

It was the commander in chief who led the nation in war. In 2008, Clinton set her sights on that job.

Run for the Presidency

Clinton won reelection to the Senate in 2006 by a wide margin. But almost before the ballots were counted, supporters were touting her as a candidate for president in 2008. She pondered the decision for months. When she asked her husband what he thought, Bill said if she believed she would be the best president of anyone running, she should go for it.

On January 20, 2007, Clinton posted a video on her website. She sat in a chair and looked straight into

Buttons adorn a Clinton supporter's T-shirt in Iowa
during the 2008 presidential campaign.

the camera. "Let's talk," she said.[10] Clinton announced
her candidacy for president of the United States. Her
primary opponents included first-term senator from
Illinois Barack Obama and former US senator from
North Carolina John Edwards. Obama had served in
the Illinois state senate before being elected to the
US Senate. Edwards had run for president in 2004,
eventually becoming his former opponent John Kerry's
running mate.

Clinton's strengths included years of experience, her
success as a US senator, her own political wisdom and
that of her husband, and the enthusiasm many women
felt for her candidacy. But Clinton did not emphasize

her gender as a qualification. At one campaign stop, she said she was not running because she was a woman, but because she was the best person to "hit the ground running in January of 2009."[11]

Clinton had a few serious flaws as a presidential candidate as well. Many Americans were uncomfortable with the idea that two families appeared to be controlling the country. If Clinton was elected president, there could be a 24-year stretch with two families in the White House: George H. W. Bush; Bill Clinton; George W. Bush; and Hillary Clinton. She also faced the negative perceptions people had formed of her when she was First Lady. She tried to turn that to her advantage, claiming her ability to stand up to propaganda had made her stronger than her Democratic opponents.

Clinton had one major strike against her. She had voted to authorize the use of troops in Iraq. As a state senator, Obama had opposed the use of force in Iraq. By 2007, the nation was mired in the war. Clinton tried to distance herself from President Bush's policies while maintaining her reputation as a Democrat strong on national security.

For most of 2007, Clinton looked poised to win the Democratic primaries. Obama was her main rival. But it seemed Clinton had the advantage on Obama. She had a vast campaign network. Clinton was expertly prepared to speak about the technicalities of any issue. Obama struggled to come up with such details and had not developed positions on key issues, such as health care.

But Obama was a fast learner who promised he would bring change to the federal government. He harnessed control of social media and was soon raising more money than Clinton. After she made a series of confusing statements about immigration, her support began slipping. Then, Clinton came in third in the Iowa caucus, while Obama, an African American, came in first in the predominantly white state. The result proved he was a serious candidate. True to form, Clinton worked even harder to win the nomination. In New Hampshire, the second primary contest, 4,000 Clinton volunteers knocked on doors.[12] Clinton won in New Hampshire, scoring an upset against Obama.

But the race was far from over. Clinton lost the South Carolina primary, and campaign donations slowed. Obama's delegate count mounted, and superdelegates began switching their votes from Clinton to Obama. Soon, Clinton had fallen too far behind to catch up. Still, she refused to concede defeat until after the final primary on June 3, 2008. One of Clinton's advisers said, "She could accept losing. She could not accept quitting."[13] Out of a possible 35.5 million votes cast, Obama won only 152,000 more than Clinton, one-half of a percentage point.[14]

The votes of the millions of Clinton supporters were crucial for an Obama victory in the general election. In August 2008, Democrats gathered in Denver, Colorado, for their national convention. Resentment lingered between the Obama and Clinton camps. But when Clinton took the stage at the convention, she began the healing process. She told the packed convention center she supported Obama. Clinton returned to the Senate, bruised but not broken, and ready to get back to work. She would not be there for long.

18 MILLION CRACKS

On June 7, 2008, Clinton conceded the Democratic nomination to Obama before an audience of thousands in the National Building Museum in Washington, DC. She addressed the dreams of all the women who had hoped to finally see a woman in the White House. "Although we weren't able to shatter that highest, hardest glass ceiling this time, thanks to you, it's got about eighteen million cracks in it. And the light is shining through like never before, filling us all with the . . . sure knowledge that the path will be a little easier next time."[15]

CHAPTER
EIGHT

MADAM SECRETARY

A few days after the 2008 election, Clinton headed to Chicago to meet with President-elect Barack Obama. When she arrived, he cut right to the chase. Obama wanted her to be his secretary of state. Clinton was stunned.

Clinton and Obama had been intense rivals in a brutal primary campaign. Now, he wanted her as a senior member of his administration. Clinton was honored but said no. She believed she could better serve her country in the Senate. Obama urged her to reconsider.

Clinton thought deeply about the offer and consulted her friends and family. When Obama called her a week later, she declined again. Obama refused to accept this. "I want to get to yes," he said.[1] Clinton barely slept that night. In the predawn darkness she finally concluded that when the president of the United States "asks you to

The secretary of state is responsible for foreign negotiations. Secretary Clinton represented the Obama administration in many countries including in Sarajevo, Bosnia, in 2010.

serve, you should say yes."[2] She called Obama the next morning and accepted the job.

On-the-Job Training

January 22, 2009, was Clinton's first day as secretary of state. She had been approved by the Senate the day before, with 94 of 100 senators voting in her favor.[3] She entered the atrium of the State Department building in Washington, DC. The huge room was lined with flags from every nation. The State Department staff gathered to welcome their new boss.

Unlike previous secretaries, Clinton had no formal diplomatic experience. Nor did she speak a foreign language. However, she understood politics, was sensitive and intuitive, and was a quick learner.

The job of secretary of state is actually three jobs: adviser to the president on foreign policy; chief diplomat of the nation; and CEO of a huge department. The work

MOTB

On July 31, 2010, Chelsea Clinton married Marc Mezvinsky. Her daughter's wedding was a day Clinton had looked forward to since Chelsea was a little girl. Between meetings with the president and ambassadors, she reviewed flower arrangements and attended dress fittings. During the wedding, she thought, "This . . . is why Bill and I . . . worked so hard for so many years to help build a better world—so Chelsea could grow up safe and happy . . . and so every other child would have the same chance."[4]

Hillary Clinton, Dorothy Rodham, and Chelsea Clinton celebrate Chelsea's wedding on July 31, 2010.

is unpredictable. One official warned Clinton that "the whole world . . . comes at you every single day."[5]

Two goals guided Clinton through her tenure at state. She wanted to restore America's global standing, damaged by the Iraq War. She also wanted to exercise smart power. This referred to the blend of military might and economic aid as a tool to influence nations.

Frequent Flier

Asia was Clinton's first destination as secretary of state. She interacted with people from all walks of life. In Japan, she met with female astronauts and the foreign minister. In Indonesia, protesters greeted her with signs reading, "America is the real terrorist."[6] In South Korea, she addressed an auditorium of students from a women's college. Meetings in communist China were tightly scripted. Over the course of seven days, Clinton made 15 speeches, gave 11 interviews, and held six town hall meetings and seven press conferences.[7]

This trip became the prototype. Over her four years at state, Clinton spent more than 2,000 hours in the air, traveling almost one million miles (1.6 million km) in a plane that was a house and office with wings.[8] The main cabin was divided into three spaces: a section for State Department staff, one for security, and the third for the press corps. Clinton encouraged everyone to dress casually and sleep as much as possible. During hours in the air, journalists saw a different side of Clinton. They watched movies together, celebrated birthdays, and shared family joys and tragedies. Staffers were surprised on the first trip abroad when Clinton joined them at a conference table instead of retiring to her private room. From that moment on, that chair was always kept vacant and known as the Hillary seat.

Successes

Some secretaries of state can point to one major diplomatic breakthrough as their legacy. Clinton had no

President Obama, Secretary Clinton, and others watch the progress of Operation Neptune Spear in the Situation Room.

such signature achievement. Instead, she accumulated a series of small but significant successes.

The United States had been hunting for bin Laden ever since the 9/11 attacks. Finally, in the spring of 2011, CIA operators located him hiding in a compound in Pakistan. For the next few weeks, Obama's team debated how to apprehend the al-Qaeda leader. As part of Obama's foreign policy team, Clinton supported a raid on the compound by a special operations team. She urged him to take the opportunity to capture bin Laden at the compound. The president agreed. Operation Neptune Spear was scheduled for May 1, the next moonless night.

Two Blackhawk helicopters transported an elite Navy SEAL special operations military team to Abbottabad, Pakistan. Secretary Clinton joined President Obama and other top advisers to watch the raid live from the White House Situation Room. One helicopter crash-landed, and the video feed vanished for 14 minutes. "That was as tense a moment as any I can remember," Clinton said later.[9] But suddenly, a US soldier spoke over the radio: Bin Laden was E-KIA, enemy killed in action. Clinton felt proud and grateful as she listened to the president inform the nation of the successful operation.

China occupied a central role in American foreign policy during Clinton's watch. The desire to foster economic ties with the country was coupled with concern over its poor human rights record. On April 25, 2012, Clinton received word from the American embassy in Beijing that Chen Guangcheng, a blind human rights activist, had escaped house arrest. He had traveled hundreds of miles on a broken foot and was seeking political asylum at the US embassy.

Clinton was scheduled to travel to China for economic meetings in a matter of days. Now she faced a dilemma: aid this one man and endanger trade talks with the Chinese government, or put economic concerns first, disregarding the principle of human rights. Clinton walked a moral tightrope. After several days of skilled and secret diplomacy, she struck a deal. Chen and his family were allowed to immigrate to the United States. The economic meetings between Clinton and Chinese authorities carried on as planned.

Myanmar was another Asian nation with an abysmal human rights record. The nation had been in the grip of a harsh military dictatorship since 1962. Aung San Suu Kyi, a democracy activist, had been under house arrest for 20 years. The United States maintained stiff economic sanctions against the country because of how

TEXTS FROM HILLARY

Two young social media wizards saw a photo of Secretary Clinton on a plane, wearing huge sunglasses and looking at her cell phone. They admired her James Bond look and used the picture to create a Tumblr account. The first entry showed an image of Obama on his phone. The caption reads, "Hey Hil, Watchu doing?" The caption under Clinton's photo reads, "Running the world."[10] So began the internet meme "Texts from Hillary." Humorous captions are paired with photos of celebrities from Meryl Streep to Mark Zuckerberg and the original photo of Clinton sporting sunglasses. Her office responded to the creators of the site with this message: "ROFL@ ur tumblr! G2g—scrunchie time. Ttyl?" meant Clinton and her office loved the meme.[11]

Aside from having fun with social media, Clinton moved the State Department into the digital world. By 2013, state had 2.6 million Twitter followers with 301 official feeds in 11 different languages.[12]

it abused its citizens. When the Myanmar government relaxed its tight control slightly in 2009, Clinton saw an opportunity to implement smart power. She promised the Myanmar regime that if it made political reforms, the United States would ease economic sanctions.

This approach, on top of the activism of Myanmar's citizens, encouraged change. In late 2010, the government released Suu Kyi and other political prisoners and scheduled new elections. In 2011, Clinton became the first US secretary of state to visit Myanmar in more than 50 years. The country held free elections in the spring of 2016, and Suu Kyi's political party won control of the government. One senior State Department official said the democratic changes in Myanmar are an example of how diplomacy could produce better results than military action.

The North African nation of Libya was another country that appeared headed for democratic change in 2011. The grassroots democracy movement known as the Arab Spring began in Tunisia in 2011 and quickly spread to Egypt and Libya. When Libyans began demanding political reforms, Muammar Gaddafi, the nation's long-standing dictator, ordered a violent crackdown. Clinton lobbied hard for a no-fly zone over Libya to prevent Gaddafi from bombing his own citizens. Others in the Obama administration disagreed, arguing the United States had no political or economic interests in Libya.

Determined to rally a coalition to implement a no-fly zone, Clinton flew 20,000 miles (32,000 km) over six days.[13] She gained support from the Security Council of the United Nations and the Arab League, a group of Arabic-speaking countries. In March 2011, the no-fly zone was enforced by an alliance of nations. In August, Gaddafi's government collapsed, and he went into hiding. Clinton stopped in Libya to meet with the country's transitional government that October. Two days later, Gaddafi was caught and executed. She told her staff, "We came. We saw. He died."[14] But this triumph was short-lived. Libya would turn into a tragedy, creating a cloud of scandal that hovered over Clinton long after.

GRANDMA HILLARY

Life is not all political strategizing for Hillary Clinton. She is a grandmother twice over. Chelsea Clinton and husband, Marc Mezvinsky, have two children: Charlotte, born in 2014, and Aidan, born in 2016. Clinton was unprepared for the experience of falling in love with her grandchildren. "It's transformational . . . it has for me been an absolutely life-changing experience."[15]

Benghazi

Following Gaddafi's death, Libya's factions jostled for power. In September 2012, Chris Stevens, the American ambassador to Libya, visited the city of Benghazi. Diplomatic staff there worked in a compound that was not highly fortified. On the evening of September 11, attackers broke in. They set fire to the structure, and black smoke billowed into a safe room where Stevens and other staff were hiding.

Clinton coordinated a response. When US troops gained control of the compound, they found the bodies of Stevens and three other deceased Americans.

Grieving herself, Clinton also had to comfort her staff and inform the families of the dead. That evening, Secretary Clinton released an official statement

BENGHAZI FLU

In December 2012, Clinton was scheduled to testify before a House committee about the Benghazi attack. However, she had a case of the flu and fainted, hitting her head on the ground. Doctors diagnosed a concussion, and Clinton's testimony had to be delayed. An editorial in the *New York Post* called her injury a "head fake," and a Florida congressman labeled her illness the "Benghazi Flu."[16] Clinton's injury was no stunt. Doctors discovered a blood clot behind her ear, and she was hospitalized for three days.

condemning the attacks. The statement implied the attackers had acted in retaliation for an online video that insulted the Muslim prophet Muhammad, a connection later found to be false.

This event occurred shortly before the 2012 presidential election. Republicans accused the administration of misleading the public to cover up a lapse in security. When Obama was reelected, Republicans shifted their attention to Clinton. She was being touted as a candidate for president in 2016.

Multiple investigations examined the failures in Benghazi. Clinton testified before Congress in January 2013. All inquiries reached the same verdict: Libya had been in chaos in 2011, and security in the Benghazi compound was lax. But neither Clinton nor anyone else in the Obama administration was to blame for the American deaths. When President Obama asked Clinton to stay on for another term at the State Department, she declined. She left office in 2013, becoming a private citizen for the first time in 30 years. But Clinton would not remain out of the spotlight for long.

CHAPTER
NINE

VICTORY
OR DEFEAT?

On April 12, 2015, two years after leaving her post as secretary of state, Clinton announced her candidacy for president. After more than a year of campaigning, she won the most votes during the Democratic primaries and became the Democratic Party's official nominee on July 26, 2016. Her popularity rose in the week following the Democratic National Convention. She led Republican nominee Donald Trump in the polls 50 to 42 percent.[1] Sometimes, Trump's provocative and controversial statements got him into trouble. But as summer turned into fall, the race tightened. Trump reined in his rhetoric. As the campaign entered its final stretch after Labor Day, Democrats grew worried.

Though Trump unsettled many voters, just as many voters disliked Clinton. Many Americans considered her aloof, secretive, and too rehearsed. Clinton set out

Trump and Clinton participated in three presidential debates leading up to the 2016 election.

to engage directly with voters, clarify her vision for America, and contrast herself with Trump.

Clinton on the Issues

According to the Pew Research Center, the top two issues for American voters in 2016 were the economy and terrorism. In August, both candidates highlighted their economic vision in Detroit, Michigan, a city where many residents were unemployed. Trump vowed to cut taxes across the board, reduce government regulations, lower taxes on business income, and end tax rules that allowed corporations to pay less.

Three days after Trump's visit, Clinton arrived in Michigan to talk about the economy. She criticized Trump's promises to average Americans. "There is a myth out there that . . . somehow, at heart, he's really on the side of the

HITTING THE AIRWAVES

Clinton's political ad campaign used Trump's own words against him. In a television ad launched in June 2016, she asked Americans if they "help each other" and if they "respect each other."[2] Then clips of Trump's speeches played on screen. In one excerpt, he tells audience members to "knock the crap" out of a protester.[3] In another, he mocks a handicapped reporter. These scenes are followed by Clinton working side-by-side with people of different ages and races, sending the message that she was the candidate of respect.

little guy. Don't believe it," she said.[4] Clinton's economic plan called for a massive investment in public infrastructure. She promised to make public colleges and universities tuition-free for middle class and poor families, and she criticized Trump's tax cuts, claiming they would benefit only the richest Americans.

First Face-to-Face

On September 26, 2016, Clinton and Trump took the stage together in the first presidential debate. Eighty-four million Americans tuned in.[3] The stakes were high. It was less than two months before the general election, and Trump and Clinton were virtually tied in the polls.

E-MAIL SCANDAL

Clinton's use of a private e-mail server while she was secretary of state came to light when Congress investigated her role in the attack on the US embassy in Benghazi. When investigators asked for her e-mails, Clinton's staff turned over 30,000 but deleted the rest, saying they were personal. This fueled controversy that Clinton was trying to cover up illegal activity. The FBI closed its first investigation into her e-mails in July 2016. Director of the FBI James Comey determined there was no evidence that Clinton had obstructed justice or behaved disloyally, but he did say she was "extremely careless."[5] However, four months later, the FBI reopened the investigation. They discovered new e-mails they had overlooked in the first investigation. The FBI concluded its second review three days before the election. They again did not find evidence of any wrongdoing.

At first, Clinton seemed stiff and sounded rehearsed as she discussed equal pay for equal work and the support that small businesses needed. The economy was Trump's strength, and he spoke clearly and calmly at first. Then, Clinton reminded viewers that Trump had rooted for the 2008 housing crisis as a benefit to his real-estate business. This comment seemed to irritate Trump. For the rest of the debate, Trump went on the defensive.

Most experts agreed that Clinton outperformed Trump. So did American voters. A week after the debate, polls showed her leading the presidential race by approximately four percentage points.[6] But there were still six weeks left until Election Day.

Election Night Arrives

Clinton's supporters gathered in Manhattan on November 8, 2016. Clinton waited out the night in a hotel in New York City with her family. The mood was hopeful. Pre-election polls had indicated that Clinton had the edge over Trump. Clinton's supporters prepared to celebrate the election of the first female president of the United States.

Clinton gave a concession speech the morning of November 9, calling for national unity.

Clinton won in Connecticut and in other democratic states early in the night. But Trump soon took the lead in Florida, a key swing state. The Clinton campaign had expected a win in Wisconsin and Michigan, but polls showed Trump winning in those states as well. It was getting to be a close race.

Early in the morning on November 9, Trump won Wisconsin. When all the votes were counted, Clinton won the popular vote, but Trump had received enough electoral votes to win the election. Clinton gave her concession speech that same morning. Although she had not won the election, Clinton had made history as the first US female presidential candidate. She crossed historic barriers, and her candidacy was a breakthrough in women's rights history.

TIMELINE

1947
Hillary Diane Rodham is born in Chicago, Illinois, on October 26.

1964
Rodham works on the presidential campaign of Republican Senator Barry Goldwater.

1969
Rodham graduates from Wellesley College and is first student in the school's history to speak at the graduation ceremony.

1973
Rodham receives a law degree from Yale Law School; she becomes an attorney for the Children's Defense Fund.

1974

Rodham does legal research for the House Judiciary Committee investigating impeachment charges against President Richard Nixon; she moves to Arkansas; she serves as assistant professor of law at the University of Arkansas until 1977.

1975

Rodham marries Bill Clinton on October 11.

1976

Rodham is a lawyer and eventually the first female partner at the Rose Law Firm in Little Rock, Arkansas, until 1992.

1980

Daughter Chelsea Clinton is born on February 27.

TIMELINE

1993
President Bill Clinton appoints Hillary Clinton to lead the Task Force on National Health Care Reform.

2000
Clinton is elected to the US Senate, representing the state of New York.

2006
Clinton is reelected to the US Senate.

2007
Clinton announces her candidacy for president on January 20.

2008
Clinton suspends her bid for president and endorses Barack Obama on June 7.

2009

Clinton is approved as secretary of state on January 21.

2013

Clinton testifies before the House Foreign Affairs Committee and the Senate Foreign Relations Committee about the 2012 attacks in Benghazi, Libya, on January 23; Clinton resigns as secretary of state on February 1.

2015

Clinton formally announces her bid for president on April 12.

2016

Clinton becomes the first female presidential nominee for a major political party at the Democratic National Convention; she loses the election on November 8.

ESSENTIAL FACTS

Date of Birth
October 26, 1947

Place of Birth
Chicago, Illinois

Parents
Hugh Rodham and Dorothy Howell Rodham

Education
Wellesley College
Yale University Law School

Marriage
William "Bill" Clinton (October 11, 1975)

Children
Chelsea

Career Highlights
Clinton served as a lawyer for the Children's Defense Fund from 1973 to 1974 and as a lawyer for the Rose Law Firm in Arkansas from 1976 to 1992. She was First Lady of Arkansas from 1979 to 1981 and again from 1983 to 1992. In 1993, she became First Lady of the United States and held that title

until her husband's second term ended in 2001. She served as US senator from New York from 2000 to 2009 and US secretary of state from 2009 to 2013.

Societal Contributions

Clinton is an advocate for health-care reform, and is an outspoken advocate for the rights of women and children around the world. She was the first woman to win the presidential nomination of a major party.

Conflicts

Clinton was alleged to have obstructed government investigations of her family's financial dealings and has been accused of inadequately protecting US embassy personnel in Libya. She has been investigated for using a personal e-mail server that did not secure confidential government documents, but she was found not to have violated the law. Still, she remained distrusted by many Americans.

Quote

"One thing that has never been a hard choice for me is serving our country. It has been the greatest honor of my life."—*Hillary Clinton,* Hard Choices. *p.xii.*

GLOSSARY

compound
A cluster of buildings surrounded by a fence or other enclosure.

conservative
Believing in small government and established social, economic, and political traditions and practices.

constituent
A voter.

convention
A gathering of members of a political party that meets to select a candidate to run for office.

cronyism
The practice of appointing friends and relatives to jobs without regard to their qualifications.

delegate
A person given power or authority to act for others.

feminist movement
A period of time between the 1950s and 1970s when women fought for political, social, and economic equality.

impeach
To charge an elected official with wrongdoing.

incumbent
Someone who currently holds public office.

lobbyist
Someone who tries to convince government officials to vote in a certain way as part of his or her job.

migrant worker
A person who moves from place to place to do seasonal work.

platform
The policies of a political party.

progressive
A person who believes in large government and supporting new ideas and ways of behaving, especially social reform.

rhetoric
Language intended to influence people, even if it may not be completely truthful.

sanction
To give official approval or permission.

superdelegate
A delegate within the Democratic Party who votes for any candidate of his or her choosing and switches allegiances up until the time the vote is held at the Democratic National Convention.

ADDITIONAL RESOURCES

Selected Bibliography

Allen, Jonathan, and Amie Parnes. *HRC: State Secrets and the Rebirth of Hillary Clinton*. New York: Broadway, 2015. Print.

Bernstein, Carl. *A Woman in Charge*. New York: Knopf, 2007. Print.

Clinton, Hillary Rodham. *Hard Choices*. New York: Simon, 2014. Print.

Clinton, Hillary Rodham. *Living History*. New York: Scribner, 2003. Print.

Further Readings

Blumenthal, Karen. *Hillary Rodham Clinton: A Woman Living History*. New York: Feiwel and Friends, 2016. Print.

Epstein, Dwayne. *Hillary Clinton*. Detroit: Lucent, 2010. Print.

Levinson, Cynthia. *Hillary Rodham Clinton: Do All the Good You Can*. New York: Harper, 2016. Print.

Websites

To learn more about Essential Lives, visit **booklinks.abdopublishing.com**. These links are routinely monitored and updated to provide the most current information available.

Places to Visit

Clinton House Museum
930 West Clinton Drive
Fayetteville, AR 72701
877-BIL-N-HIL
http://www.clintonhousemuseum.org
This museum is the first home of Bill and Hillary Clinton. It contains personal and political memorabilia from their lives.

Edward M. Kennedy Institute for the US Senate
210 Morrissey Boulevard
Boston, MA 02125
617-740-7000
http://www.emkinstitute.org
The Institute for the US Senate includes a re-creation of the Senate chamber in which visitors can vote on the legislation of the day.

National First Ladies' Library
Saxton McKinley House
331 South Market Avenue
Canton, OH 44702
330-452-0876
http://www.firstladies.org
The site includes the family home of First Lady Ida Saxton McKinley and the Education and Research Center with exhibits on America's First Ladies, a Victorian theater, and a research library.

SOURCE NOTES

Chapter 1. Shattering the Glass Ceiling

1. Krishnadev Calamur. "It's Official: Hillary Clinton Announces Presidential Run." *The Two-Way*. NPR, 12 Apr. 2015. Web. 25 Jul. 2016.

2. Scott Pelley. "The Democratic Ticket." *60 Minutes*. CBSNews, 24 Jul. 2016. Web. 25 Jul. 2016.

3. PBS NewsHour. "Watch Hillary Clinton's Full Speech at the 2016 Democratic National Convention." *YouTube*. YouTube, 28 Jul. 2016. Web. 29 Jul. 2016.

4. Ibid.

5. Katie Hicks. "Chelsea Clinton DNC Speech Transcript 2016." *Vox*. Vox Media, 28 Jul. 2016. Web. 29 Jul. 2016.

Chapter 2. No Room for Cowards

1. Karen Blumenthal. *Hillary Rodham Clinton: A Woman Living History*. New York: Feiwel, 2016. Print. 28.

2. Hillary Rodham Clinton. *Living History*. New York: Simon, 2003. Print. 162.

3. Ibid. 11.

4. Carl Bernstein. *A Woman in Charge*. New York: Knopf, 2007. Print. 15.

5. Ibid. 30.

6. Hillary Rodham Clinton. *Living History*. New York: Simon, 2003. Print. 29.

7. Ibid. 24.

8. Carl Bernstein. *A Woman in Charge*. New York: Knopf, 2007. Print. 34.

9. Hillary Rodham Clinton. *Living History*. New York: Simon, 2003. Print. 22.

Chapter 3. The Making of an Activist

1. Hillary Rodham Clinton. *Living History*. New York: Simon, 2003. Print. 27.

2. Ibid. 27.

3. Ibid. 33.

4. Carl Bernstein. *A Woman in Charge*. New York: Knopf, 2007. Print. 53.

5. Ibid. 51.

6. "Vietnam War Deaths and Casualties by Month." *The Names of Vietnam War Personnel: 1945 to 1975*. American War Library, 27 Nov. 2008. Web. 10 Jul. 2016.

7. Hillary Rodham Clinton. *Living History*. New York: Simon, 2003. Print. 35.

8. Ibid. 36.

9. Carl Bernstein. *A Woman in Charge*. New York: Knopf, 2007. Print. 58–9.

10. Hillary Rodham Clinton. *Living History*. New York: Simon, 2003. Print. 43.

11. Karen Blumenthal. *Hillary Rodham Clinton: A Woman Living History*. New York: Feiwel, 2016. Print. 66.

12. Hillary Rodham Clinton. *Living History*. New York: Simon, 2003. Print. 38.

13. Ibid. 50–51.

Chapter 4. Love and Politics

1. Carl Bernstein. *A Woman in Charge*. New York: Knopf, 2007. Print. 79.
2. Ibid.
3. Hillary Rodham Clinton. *Living History*. New York: Simon, 2003. Print. 57.
4. Carl Bernstein. *A Woman in Charge*. New York: Knopf, 2007. Print. 83.
5. Ibid. 87.
6. Hillary Rodham Clinton. *Living History*. New York: Simon, 2003. Print. 68.
7. Ibid. 69.
8. Carl Bernstein. *A Woman in Charge*. New York: Knopf, 2007. Print. 109.
9. Ibid. 115.
10. Hillary Rodham Clinton. *Living History*. New York: Simon, 2003. Print. 74.
11. Carl Bernstein. *A Woman in Charge*. New York: Knopf, 2007. Print. 123.

Chapter 5. Political Battles in the Razorback State

1. Carl Bernstein. *A Woman in Charge*. New York: Knopf, 2007. Print. 130–1.
2. Hillary Rodham Clinton. *Living History*. New York: Simon, 2003. Print. 77–78.
3. Karen Blumenthal. *Hillary Rodham Clinton: A Woman Living History*. New York: Feiwel, 2016. Print. 126.
4. Carl Bernstein. *A Woman in Charge*. New York: Knopf, 2007. Print. 144–145.
5. Karen Blumenthal. *Hillary Rodham Clinton: A Woman Living History*. New York: Feiwel, 2016. Print. 132–133.
6. Carl Bernstein. *A Woman in Charge*. New York: Knopf, 2007. Print. 165.
7. Hillary Rodham Clinton. *Living History*. New York: Simon, 2003. Print. 93.
8. Carl Bernstein. *A Woman in Charge*. New York: Knopf, 2007. Print. 167.
9. Hillary Rodham Clinton. *Living History*. New York: Simon, 2003. Print. 94.
10. Bernstein, Carl. *A Woman in Charge*. New York: Knopf, 2007. Print. 208–209.
11. Carl Bernstein. *A Woman in Charge*. New York: Knopf, 2007. Print. 199–200.
12. Ibid. 206.
13. Karen Blumenthal. *Hillary Rodham Clinton: A Woman Living History*. New York: Feiwel, 2016. Print. 168–169.

Chapter 6. White House Work

1. Carl Bernstein. *A Woman in Charge*. New York: Knopf, 2007. Print. 219.
2. Ibid.
3. Hillary Rodham Clinton. *Living History*. New York: Simon, 2003. Print. 258–259.
4. Ibid. 259.
5. Karen Blumenthal. *Hillary Rodham Clinton: A Woman Living History*. New York: Feiwel, 2016. Print. 186.
6. Carl Bernstein. *A Woman in Charge*. New York: Knopf, 2007. Print. 304.
7. Karen Blumenthal. *Hillary Rodham Clinton: A Woman Living History*. New York: Feiwel, 2016. Print. 200–201.

SOURCE NOTES CONTINUED

8. Alan Gathright. "Did Hillary Clinton Win Health Care for 8 Million Children as First Lady?" *PolitiFact Colorado*. PolitiFact, 15 Feb. 2016. Web. 27 Feb. 2016.

9. Hillary Rodham Clinton. *Living History*. New York: Simon, 2003. Print. 141.

10. Amy Chozik. "Hillary Clinton's Beijing Speech on Women Resonates 20 Years Later." *New York Times*. New York Times, 5 Sep. 2016. Web. 20 Sep. 2016.

11. Karen Blumenthal. *Hillary Rodham Clinton: A Woman Living History*. New York: Feiwel, 2016. Print. 210.

12. Ibid. 257.

13. Hillary Rodham Clinton. *Living History*. New York: Simon, 2003. Print. 469.

Chapter 7. Pursuit of Dreams

1. Hillary Rodham Clinton. *Living History*. New York: Simon, 2003. Print. 501.

2. Josh Getlin. "Hillary Clinton Formally Announces Senate Campaign." *SFGate*. Los Angeles Times, 7 Feb. 2000. Web. 16 Jul. 2016.

3. "Hillary Clinton Elected to Senate From New York." *New York Times*. New York Times, 8 Nov. 2000. Web. 12 Jun. 2016.

4. Susan Davis. "Hillary Clinton's Senate Years Provide Insight into How She Might Govern." *NPR*. NPR, 28 Apr. 2016. Web. 17 Jul. 2016.

5. Carl Bernstein. *A Woman in Charge*. New York: Knopf, 2007. Print. 548.

6. Karen Blumenthal. *Hillary Rodham Clinton: A Woman Living History*. New York: Feiwel, 2016. Print. 303.

7. Ibid.

8. "Congressional Record: Proceedings and Debates of the 107th Congress Second Session." vol. 148. Washington, DC: United States Government Printing Office, n.d. *Google Book Search*. Web. 17 July 2016. p. 20,435.

9. Karen Blumenthal. *Hillary Rodham Clinton: A Woman Living History*. New York: Feiwel, 2016. Print. 306.

10. Dan Balz and Haynes Johnson. *The Battle for America 2008*. New York: Viking, 2009. Print. 53.

11. Katharine Q. Seelye and Ben Werschku. "A Look Back at 'Hillary 2008.'" *Times Video*. New York Times Company, 4 Jun. 2008. Web. 17 Jul. 2016.

12. Dan Balz and Haynes Johnson. *The Battle for America 2008*. New York: Viking, 2009. Print. 137.

13. Ibid. 216.

14. Ibid. 217.

15. Jonathan Allen and Amie Parnes. *HRC: State Secrets and the Rebirth of Hillary Clinton*. New York: Crown, 2014. Print. 31.

Chapter 8. Madam Secretary

1. Hillary Rodham Clinton. *Hard Choices*. New York: Simon, 2013. Print. 18.

2. Ibid.

3. Kate Phillips. "Senate Confirms Clinton as Secretary of State." *New York Times*. New York Times, 21 Jan. 2009. Web. 1 Jul. 2016.

4. Hillary Rodham Clinton. *Hard Choices*. New York: Simon, 2013. Print. 81–82.

5. US Department of State. "Secretary Clinton Swearing In Ceremony." *YouTube*. YouTube, 12 Feb. 2009. Web. 1 Jul. 2016.

6. Kim Ghattas. *The Secretary: A Journey with Hillary Clinton from Beirut to the Heart of American Power*. New York: Henry Holt, 2013. Print. 37.

7. Ibid. 50.

8. Ibid. 40.

9. Hillary Rodham Clinton. *Hard Choices*. New York: Simon, 2013. Print. 195.

10. "Texts from Hillary." *Texts from Hillary*. Tumblr, 4 Apr. 2012. Web. 23 Jul. 2016.

11. "Texts from Hillary." *Texts from Hillary*. Tumblr, 10 Apr. 2012. Web. 23 Jul. 2016.

12. Hillary Rodham Clinton. *Hard Choices*. New York: Simon, 2013. Print. 551.

13. Karen Blumenthal. *Hillary Rodham Clinton: A Woman Living History*. New York: Feiwel, 2016. Print. 357.

14. Ibid.

15. Dan Merica. "Chelsea Clinton Gives Birth to a Baby Boy, Her Second Child." *CNN Politics*. Cable News Network, 20 Jun. 2016. Web. 18 Jul. 2016.

16. Jonathan Allen and Amie Parnes. *HRC: State Secrets and the Rebirth of Hillary Clinton*. New York: Crown, 2014. Print. 341.

Chapter 9. Victory or Defeat?

1. Hannah Hartig, et al. "Poll: Clinton Support Spikes Following Democratic Convention." *NBC News*. NBC, 2 Aug. 2016. Web. 18 Sep. 2016.

2. Josh Haskell. "Clinton Frames First General Election Ad as 'Choice About Who We Are as a Nation.'" *ABC News*. ABC News Network, 12 Jun. 2016. Web. 12 Aug. 2016.

3. Ibid.

4. Amy Chozick and Alan Rappeport. "In Michigan, Hillary Clinton Calls Donald Trump Enemy of 'the Little Guy.'" *New York Times*. New York Times, 11 Aug. 2016. Web. 12 Aug. 2016.

5. Lauren Carroll. "The GOP's Opening over Hillary Clinton's Email." *PolitiFact*. Tampa Bay Times, 19 Jul. 2016. Web. 4 Oct. 2016.

6. "Monday, October 3." *Real Clear Politics*. RealClearPolitics.com, n.d. Web. 21 Oct. 2016.

INDEX

ABOUT THE AUTHOR

Judy Dodge Cummings is a writer and former history teacher from Wisconsin. Her books include *The American Revolution: Experience the Battle for Independence*, *Exploring Polar Regions*, and *Human Migration: Investigate the Global Journey of Humankind*. She is a political junkie and has voted in every election since her eighteenth birthday.